MW01234318

GOLF SWING

*A Modern Guide for Beginners to
Understand Golf Swing Mechanics, Improve
Your Technique and Play Like the Pros*

Norman Delgado

TABLE OF CONTENTS

Introduction

Congratulations on purchacing *Golf Swing,* and thank you for doing so.

For any amateur golfer, the worst fear is embarrassing themselves during the game. And it can be overwhelming for them to learn so many things at once. But my aim in this book is to make the learning process easier and to show you how you can achieve that perfect and professional golf swing with just a few simple steps.

Throughout the book, you will find that everything has been systematically explained, and special exercises have also been included that will help you hone your skills and improve your technique. The key concepts that you need to learn to improve your golf swing have all been covered as comprehensively as possible. An improved and practiced swing can take you high up your golfing experience. But remember that you will meet success only if you show dedication in these initial stages. You need to familiarize yourself with all the techniques and movements, and then, you will not have to worry about your golf swing for years to come!

There is one thing that you all need to keep in mind – the longer you play golf and swing your club in the wrong way, the more effort you will have to put into correcting the swing. And the good news is that it's not too difficult if you know what to do.

There are plenty of books on this subject on the market. Thanks again for choosing this one! Every effort was made to ensure it is full of as much useful information as possible, please enjoy!

Chapter 1: Basics of Golf

If you want to know more about honing your golf skill, you must start learning the golf basics. Once you master these, you will be on your way to becoming a pro golfer. In this chapter, I will talk about the basics of golf that you should know and master.

Important Points for Beginners

For becoming a pro golfer, you need to develop your understanding, skills, and abilities. Here are the basics of golf that will help you to do so:

Nailing the Basic Fundamentals

It is possible to spot a pro golfer even before they hit the golf ball. That is because they have a good stance, grip, and posture. They also have a pre-shot routine, responsible for helping them in repeating these things every time. You need to follow some guidelines while gripping the golf club. Then you need to step into the golf ball using one leg and then bow. Lastly, you need to adjust your weight in a way that balances your body weight.

Understanding the Concept behind Getting the Ball into the Air

Beginners often struggle to get the ball into the air. The basic concept behind getting the ball up in the air is that you should hit the ground. You need to have a good posture, bend from the hips, and extend both of your arms into the ground while you swing, just like how you throw a ball.

Knowing How Far the Clubs Go

It is necessary to have a clear idea about how far your clubs can go. Make a list of the clubs that you have. Whenever you hit a good shot, measure the distance and note it down on the list. It will help you to have a clear idea.

Having a Reliable Fairway Club

If you are not comfortable with your club, it can affect your game. Every golfer has some preferences when it comes to the comfort level with the clubs. You should find out a club with which you are comfortable. Also, make sure that

it goes a decent distance. It will build your
confidence, and you will have fun too.

Hitting a Basic Golf Chip
Even as a beginner, you must have the ability to
hit the simple golf chip. The shot doesn't
necessarily need to be perfect, especially if you
are a beginner. The main goal is to make you
have a go-to shot. Hold the club, bend towards
your target, and then make a putting motion.
Practice this a few times until you get
comfortable with it.

Short Game Priority Order
Risk management is crucial. You have to choose
the right shot. When the motion is small, the
chances of error are also less. You have to putt
whenever you can. In case you can't putt, you
should chip. You can pitch if necessary.

Hitting a Basic Bunker Shot
Beginner golfers struggle at sand shorts. As I
have already mentioned, you should hit the
ground if you want to hit the ball up. It means
that you need to override any instinct that you
have to lift the ball, and you need to hit the sand.
You can also try digging your feet into the sand.

Being Well-Equipped with the Necessary Tools
It is crucial to be well-equipped with all the
necessary equipment and tools that you will
need. You need to have a ball marker, tees, 6 to
12 golf balls, and a golf glove (optional).

Learning Putting

A golfer needs to learn how to put. It is challenging, but it is also fun. You will be bowing from your hips, your eyes should be over the ball, and your arms must hang from the shoulder. Your backstroke length is responsible for controlling the distance. If the strokes are small, then the putting swing will be slow. Whereas, if the strokes are large, the putting swing will be fast. Use your feet to regulate the size of the stroke.

Learning the Rules and Etiquette

Apart from working on your skills, focus on learning all the basic rules and etiquette. You should know how to drop the ball, how to take relief from a lie that is unplayable, etc.

Importance of Golf Swing

The action by which a golf player hits the ball is known as a golf swing. It is a very complex motion, and it involves your entire body. The two most critical elements of a golf swing are timing and power.

A good golf swing depends on three factors:

- ***Posture*** – Having a proper posture is a must if you want a good golf swing. You should set up and move in an athletic and balanced fashion. You should have a good stance. Your back should be relatively straight, and your legs should be slightly bent. The stance's width must be somewhat equal to the width of your shoulder, and your arms should hang free.

- *Alignment* – At address, your body must be positioned parallelly with the target line. You can adjust the stance for different shots, but generally, both the stance and your body must go parallelly with the target line.

- *Grip* – You can grip the club in various ways. Usually, golfers use any one of these three grips – baseball grip, interlocking grip, and overlapping grip.

There are three types of strokes:

- *Chip* – Golfers use this type of stroke when the ball is within a short range around the green. You can use any club for chipping, but it is better to use chippers (specialized clubs meant for chipping).

- **Pitch** – This stroke is for hitting the ball high from short distances. Golfers use a high lofted club for pitching.

- **Putt** – Golfers use this type of stroke for putting the ball in the hole when the ball is already present in the green or is on the fringe of the green.

The entire game depends on the golf swing, so a golfer needs to know all the technicalities of the golf swing. The golf swing's goal is to transfer the kinetic energy into the clubhead. When the clubhead comes in contact with the ball, it transmits the kinetic energy into the ball and sends it into flight.

Chapter 2: Importance of Balance in Golf Swing

You must have heard that balance in a golf swing is extremely important, but do you know why is it so? To obtain maximum potential while swinging your golf, one of the important factors is balance. Yes, that is how important balance is! I will walk you through the importance of balance in detail in the next section but let us have a quick peek at how and why balance plays such a major role in a golf swing. If your body becomes unbalanced while taking a swing, the focus will be reverted towards bringing back your body to balance. In other words, the body will work on itself to compensate for the lost balance, causing many variables. These variables will likely distract your focus from taking the swing, thus causing you to take a shot that is not the best.

Whereas if your body is in a state of complete balance, you can take a good shot as no variables can distract your focus. Thus to have maximum effectiveness, it is necessary to have your body in a state of equilibrium. That way, your body will not try to work on compensating for the imbalance and allow you to exploit your maximum potential while taking a golf swing.

Now let us look at what we mean when we say balance concerning golf swings and discuss why it is so important to attain a perfect swing.

Why Is Balance So Important for the Perfect Swing?

Many people will argue that golf is more of an art than science! I will not get into that argument but would agree that golf is a form of art where a solid swing is a blessing for the golfer and the spectators. When the torso, arms, hands, feet, and legs are all in harmony, the shot taken looks clean and solid. This harmony among all the moving parts of the body is what balance implies concerning swings in the game of golf. Naturally, when this harmony is missing, the swing no longer remains solid but becomes loose. Not only that, in the absence of proper balance, the important checks that golfers live for, like accuracy and distance, can also not be attained. Some may point out that they have attained both accuracy and distance without really bothering about the balance. It is just mere luck that allowed golfers to attain those points or objectives without balance, and they can not attain it consistently. The major areas of concern that will be faced by every golfer and cause them to lose their balance are:

1. Losing their balance due to overswinging

2. Maintaining balance while swinging for the tee shot

3. Lifting the heel intentionally while backswing

Losing Balance Due to Overswinging

The most common reason that can cause a golfer to lose their balance is overswinging. Amateur golfers, as well as seasoned golfers, are likely to overswing their golf in an attempt to cause the ball to reach farther. Overswinging refers to when you are taking your golf club farther behind your head or back in an attempt to address the ball with full potential.

Although a golfer feels like they can hit the ball with all their might by overswinging the club, what happens for real is that the players lose their balance, and their shot gets affected adversely.

You may experiment with your golf swing but avoid overswinging. If you fail to realize when your attempt is changing to overswinging, just look for the signs. One of the most common signs that you are overswinging is that it will start bending when your arm is at the top of the swing. This is a clear indication that you must adjust the swing before finally taking the shot.

A golfer gets unbalanced while overswinging due to the tilting of their torso forward as they continue to move or sway their arm farther behind their head. This pulls the body off of balance.

Mastering the art of attaining the perfect swing to reach far distances is a challenge that even many professional golfers fail to attempt. If you like the technique and gameplay of golfer Davis Love III, then you must have noticed that he has evolved, and so has his swinging over the years. You, too, need to do the same if you want to master the art of playing golf. Practice and look for ways to sway your golf compactly without really hampering the accuracy, effectiveness, and any sacrifice in the distance.

Understanding the Role of Balance While Swinging the Tee Shot

Stance plays another major role in the golfer's game. Let us consider the tee shot. While taking the tee shot, the balance can be maintained by separating your feet wide apart. In the case of tee shots, maintaining balance is fairly easy as most of the time, the golfer will be mounted on a smooth surface.

One easy way of attaining balance while addressing the ball during the tee shot is to have a wide stance. A narrow stance leads to losing balance easily due to the shift of weight while swinging your golf. It also leads to the golfer missing the target.

In order to balance the body, the stance can be a little wider than the shoulder. If you have been playing golf for some time, you will know that while taking the backswing, the weight gets shifted. If we consider a right-hand golfer while taking a backswing, he will need to switch his weight from the left leg to the right leg and the opposite legs for left-handed golfers. Now the key to maintaining balance in this situation is to ensure that the weight is not allowed to slide past the right foot.

Here a question may arise, and that is, "Shall we make our stance wider to ensure the balance is maintained?" This is a plothole where golfers tend to slip into. As soon as they hear that a narrow stance can cause them to lose balance and lose the target, they start widening their stance and not realizing that distancing the feet too much away from each other is also not the right choice and also has an adverse effect. The stance has to be kept at an optimal to maintain equilibrium.

I understand that some of you may still be wondering that what is wrong with having a wide stance, right? So let me tell you about all the disadvantages you will have to face if you distance your feet wide apart.

The disadvantages faced due to excessively wide stance are:

1. ***Not being able to attain a proper or good finish position*** - A good finish position allows a golfer to take good shots. Thus it goes without saying that it is always good to end up in a good finish position. What can be considered as a proper or good finish position? When the maximum weight is successfully shifted to the golfer's left foot and the toe of the right shoe touches the turf. This goes without saying that when you do not end in a proper finishing position, you are stuck on the right side at the back, you will miss taking a good swing. Although not being able to attain a proper finishing position has other driving factors as well, taking a wide stance is one of them. So one of the areas that you need to work on is shortening your stance if you are facing trouble with having a proper finishing position.

2. ***Making a fat hit*** - While golfers do make fat hits from time to time, it is not considered good when a golfer starts hitting fat shots now and then. When you realize that you are hitting the turf quite often, even when you are playing with short golfs, understand that there is a problem. The problem is mostly in your stance. When you take a stance where your feet are extremely far away from each other, you lose your balance. And due to that, even though you are not planning on it, you take a fat hit. Making fat hits frequently is not something that any golfer wants. Thus to avoid the pattern where you are hitting the turf more frequently, avoid placing your feet too far away from each other. Wondering how does a wide stance drives you towards making fat shots? In order to make your golf club have clean contact with the ball, you have to be able to move your lower body with the swing. This can be achieved with the help of the legs actively supporting you while the golf club makes the downswing. Now having a wider stance will only cause the legs to not support the golfer during the downswing, and thus making the golfer hit the ground even before hitting the ball.

3. ***During the backswing, not being able to make a full turn*** - The degree

of a full or proper backswing is determined by the personal flexibility of the golfers. However, each golfer needs to do their best to attain a certain degree of backswing. When you are taking a stance with the feet farther apart from each other, the flexibility to take a proper backswing is diminished. You can try this for yourself and validate the truth of the statement. Take a backswing first with your stance being at an optimum; by optimum, I mean that the feet should be distanced only as much a part as the shoulders are.

Apart from the points mentioned above, there is another disadvantage with maintaining a wide stance and that is slipping during the backswing. Not included this as a point since it is more of a rare occurrence than the rest of the events. This rare occurrence may take place if the right foot, which is the backfoot for right-handed golfers, is placed far in the right. In that situation, the leg will not be capable of taking any bodyweight on them, and due to that, the leg will likely not be able to be held in place. The back leg plays a major role when it comes to taking a proper golf swing, so in the case where the leg (right leg for right-handed golfers and left leg for left-handed golfers) is not held in place, the swing will be thrown off, and the golfer is likely to slip.

The chances of the golfer losing grip on the ground while swinging the golf from back to downswing and slipping are much higher when he or she is playing on a slope or is in an area that is not dry and has some dew or moisture. Although the event is not as frequent and can be avoided if played on dry and flat ground, it can still happen. Thus, to completely avoid the event from occurring, the stance should not be made excessively broad.

Now that we have discussed the importance of balance while taking a stance or during the golf swing, you must be eager about how to find a proper stance for yourself. The best way of finding a good stance is through heat and trial.

Lifting the Heel Intentionally While on Top of the Backswing

Some golfers have a habit of lifting their heels as soon as they reach or are about to reach the top of the backswing. Players usually do this in an attempt to generate additional power while trying to address the ball. It might also be done with the hope of lengthening the sway.

However, if any golfer raises their heels too high up then, it is a cause for them to lose their balance. If you or any other golfer lifts their heel too high up from the ground, then it might become a little difficult for you or them to land the heels back in the same spot from where they started while at the beginning of addressing the ball. This will cause them to lose their chance at hitting a perfect clubface square, and the purpose of lifting the heel will also be dissolved.

Thus it should be noticed while practicing, worked on, and ensured that you are not raising your heels too high up while at the top of the back-sway. Keep working on the area and notice that you will have a consistent footwalk within few months, which is important for consistent swings.

Tips on Improving Your Balance

Balance is important in golf as it allows the lower half of your body to have stability during the golf swing. The key to achieving balance while taking a swing is by maintaining harmony between the swing and the body movement or the turning of the body. Having the two factors in sync is the best way to score the perfect solid shot, which is consistent.

As easy as it may sound, the task of maintaining a proper balance is not that easy to attain. Some golfers may still find it difficult to be able to maintain a balance while playing golf. So here are some tips for all the golfers out there to help them maintain a good balance while playing golf:

1. ***The Half Swing*** - No matter how hard someone tries, they may accidentally end up swinging too hard. This causes them to miss their chance of striking a solid shot. To avoid this from happening, a golfer can make half swings. How to do a half swing? It is pretty easy. Simply cross your right foot over your left foot. This helps maintain the overall balance and ensures that you are not overswinging and then taking the shot.

2. ***Play dummy shots with short iron before taking your stance*** - While playing the tee, the most common mistake is to have a wide stance. Some players also make the mistake of taking a narrow stance. To fix these habits, you can adopt another habit. Before the actual stance, try playing few dummy shots with a short iron. This leads you to get the hang of the short iron for a while, and then when you

go back to taking the stance that you have practiced for the game, you feel balanced. Not just that, your body turns, and the sway of the club is in harmony.

There are many other ways of improving your body balance while playing golf; try taking help of them as well. But for now, I hope these two tips come in handy for you and helps you to become a better golf player who has the balance under his control.

Practicing the shots and planning strategies is not enough if you want to become a great golf player. It also requires huge efforts to maintain the overall balance of the body. A balanced lower half of the body during the golf swing allows the player to play the game with his or her maximum potential.

Chapter 3: How to Use Momentum for the Perfect Swing?

Golf is considered a sport that requires a natural flair and is not everybody's cup of tea, but you will be surprised to know that all it requires is some understanding of the laws of nature, and it can help beginners improve their swing and thereby the shot-making. What looks like a work of divine hand when one strikes the ball on the green turf and launches it in the air to make it land perfectly is the work of physics that Newton's laws of motion can explain like force, momentum, impulse, and torque. Let us then begin by first understanding these aforementioned factors.

Torque, which may be defined as the force of rotation that changes the rate at which an object rotates, is one of the most important factors. It can be measured by multiplying force and distance. Applying this to the context of golfing indicates the rotation of the shoulders during the backswing and the position of the hips as well during the swing. The drive attained is directly proportional to the turning force applied. Therefore, if you apply more turning force to the swing, the drive will be faster and more powerful. It is similar to the principle, which makes unscrewing a bolt with a spanner easier than barehanded.

Impulse is another important factor that measures the effect of the force acting over time. It is calculated by multiplying force and time. This impulse brings about a change in the momentum and sends the ball flying when hit by the club. A force is applied back to the club by the ball, which then sightly slows its speed down after impact. The torque of the swing produces this force and hence becomes important in generating a powerful drive. Studies have revealed that more than the power of wrists, it the rapid build-up of power or the momentum generated that causes a good swing.

Learning to Coil

In the context of golf, the term coiling is used to refer to the rotation of the body as while making a strike, the upper body rotates or what is termed as 'coils' against the resistance that the lower body provides. It is this technique of coiling used that differentiates between a pro and an amateur golfer. Our bodies work like a coil that gets stretched at the top of the backswing and then prepares to spring back through the downswing. The angular difference between the torso and lower part of the body determines the perfection of a shot while making a backswing. It helps to generate a good speed when uncoiling through a downswing. Here are some instructions that will guide you in learning to coil for power.

It is important to wind the upper body while making a backswing to ensure a powerful and solid ball striking. One might think that they need to make a big turn off the ball or make a swing back till the ball on the ground and shaft is in a parallel position, but what the feeling that one needs to get is as if storing up energy while taking the club back just like how armies prepare to launch a catapult into the position of firing. The aim must be to store up energy on the backswing that can be released once you start down to hit towards your target. An effective exercise to help build up the energy is to stand in your position with your club with your hands drooping towards the ground. Then, cross your wrists over each other in a way that the back of your two hands is in contact with each other.

After making sure that your lower body is steady, attempt to rotate the right side of your body away from the target and while doing so, counter this movement with your left arm. As a result of this, an opposing force that will arise in your body will give you a sensation of coiling in the back muscles and core. Another benefit of practicing this exercise is that it helps maintain the left arm's posture, helping to keep it in an extended position. It often happens that beginners fail to keep the position of the lead arm, and it collapses while making a backswing. It then deters one from hitting the ball powerfully. The combined effect of maintaining the extended position of the left arm and the upper body coil puts one in a position where they can hit the ball with a good drive and powerfully.

The posture and movement of the hips are also important while making a shot. Learning the science of making a proper and powerful backswing will ensure that you are ready to handle the first move well. It is important to do and hold a winding drill above for a few seconds, and you will be able to feel a stretch in your back muscles. In this stretched position, you have to begin to rotate your lower body in the direction of the target. You will gradually begin to feel your body weight shifting onto your left side. While making a swing, your hips should ideally turn forward before releasing the top-of-backswing position. Once you get a feel of this, keep practicing some shots to recreate the same movement.

Mastering Weight Transfer

There are many different ways to hit the golf ball, but in all the different methods, the technique of transferring the weight plays an important role as it is key to generating a powerful shot. Amateur golfers may think that all that power needed to make a long shot may be generated using the strength of the arms, but only a limited amount of power can be generated with strong and steady hands. Without a good weight shift or weight transfer, it is difficult to hit the ball with power as, though arm strength may wield that power, the main source of power comes from the movement of the body weight from back to front.

The difficult part of weight shifting in the golf swing is that it is not visible to our eyes.

When a golfer hits a ball, we can easily see where the central position of their body mass is as the back, and forth movement is visible but assessing the weight transfer with naked eyes is difficult. It is similar to how when one hits a ball, they might finish the stroke with a heel in the air, but there may be still a lot of weight on that foot that is not visible to us. The technique of weight transfer also demands the right timing to do so. If one does not take care of the timing of weight shifting during the golf swing, they might find it difficult to make good contact with the ball or hit it in the right direction and maintain balance. Read on to find out how to make a perfect weight transfer and hit a far and straight shot.

Let us first understand what weight transfer is in the golf swing. Weight transfer, or what many call weight shift in the golf swing, is the change of weight during the sequence of the swing from one foot to the other. People often confuse it with the center of gravity or the mass of the body as they are easily noticeable when compared to weight shift. Let us understand weight shift in terms of the percentage of body weight on each foot. A good place to start would be with equal body weight on each foot, meaning fifty percent of the weight on each foot when you are standing at the address position. Your body weight will automatically shift to a higher percentage from the backfoot in the backswing to the front foot as it goes downswing.

Now let us understand the importance of weight transfer in the golf swing – Golf is a sport that does not require much muscular power but rather requires technique and timing to obtain maximum results. Weight transfer is one such technique which when made at the correct time, enables a player to release maximum power during the golf swing. Understanding this in comparison to pitching in baseball may be easy for those who are new to golf. In baseball, the pitcher cannot rely completely on just having muscular arms to throw the ball hard but relies on the power that he uses pushing off the rubber in the direction of the home plate and the stretch or flexibility of his arm motion. Golf is extremely similar to this.

Weight shift, therefore, besides allowing you to blow up your weight through the golf ball, also lets you turn better and generate a good length while making a swing. You can enhance your body to turn better and pile up energy that can be concentrated in the golf ball by shifting your weight from one foot to another. Weight transfer is much like hammering a nail into a wall. The proportions of the object hitting the nail will definitely make a difference, but it is easier to drive it in the wall with a hammer because of its weight than with a toothbrush or a similar object. Your body weight plays a similar role in a golf swing, which, with the correct technique, can be used to your advantage to substantially increase your power without putting any extraordinary effort.

The correct way to transfer weight can be divided into three steps – the address position, transition, and weight shift, and finish position.

- ***The Address Position*** - As mentioned before, a good position to start is with an equal percentage of weight on each foot. When you begin to swing, your weight automatically will move to your back foot, and your body mass will naturally move to that side of your body that you use to make the swing. Your body mass, when your hands are near your waist, is the farthest away from your center of gravity, but it should not interfere with the weight

34

shift while your arms sway to the top of your backswing. Concentrate on shifting the weight to your back foot without swaying your body backward. Seventy-five percent of your body weight should be on your back foot at the end of your swing when done correctly.

- ***Transition and Weight Shift*** – The first impact after completion of the backswing is the weight shift in the lower body, which starts at the hips. It is through the impact of the weight transfer in the lower body that the upper body naturally follows a weight shift. Unlike what many believe, the address position is not the same as the impact position. In the address position, the majority of your body weight should be on the front foot, while at impact, the majority of your body weight should be on the hindfoot.

- ***Finish Position*** – In the final position, after you have hit the ball, you should ideally be having about ninety percent of your weight on the front foot, and if so, it means that the weight transfer throughout the process was accurate.

Amateur golfers are prone to making common
mistakes when it comes to weight transfer, like
there may not be any weight transfer at all,
which can be identified if one finishes with equal
weight on both feet. The other common mistake
is hanging back. That is, they fail to transfer the
weight back forward from the back foot. Swaying
or rocking too much back and forth, which
amateurs often do thinking that it would help to
gain much power and shift their weight through
the ball, but for that, the body does not need to
move in the direction of weight shifting. It can be
done without vigorous movements. Moving the
body back and forth only results in difficulties
like making contact with the ball or may disrupt
the timing of the impact position, thereby
making it difficult to hit the ball. The back
shoulders should not be making much
movement when transferring the weight. It
should move a notable amount in the downswing
and the finishing position.

You may follow these tips to improve your weight transfer in your golf swing.
Hold a basketball or a medicine ball and swing it in the manner you would swing the golf club and then release it at impact. Try to make a straight and long throw. If you manage to throw it far, you will know that you have aced the weight transfer, and then you can do the same while playing golf.

For the next exercise, take a sand wedge and place its face under your back heel. Try some shots, and you will see that the sand wedge will drop each time to the ground before you make an impact as your back heel will be lifted slightly. This means you are transferring the weight correctly, and if the sack drops after the impact, it means you are stuck a little too long on your back foot.

Another simple and quick exercise is to try and tap your back toe on the ground after hitting shots without losing balance. You can be sure of a correct weight transfer if you manage to do this right after your short, and if it takes you a few seconds more to lift your heel after finishing the shot, it means that your back foot still has too much weight.

The prerequisites of playing golf and other sports are somewhat different. Golfing is a sport that depends a lot on technique. If you understand the concepts of physics behind it as explained in this chapter and practice the tips suggested, you will in no time transition from an amateur to a professional and hit perfect shots.

Chapter 4: Tips for a Consistent Golf Swing

As you already know, a golf swing is the most important part of golf. The entire game depends on it. A golf swing is an action by which a golfer hits the ball. This complex motion involves the player's entire body. Power and timing are the two key elements of a golf swing. There are three types of strokes – putt, pitch, and chip all of which have already been discussed prior in this book.

Building consistency is a must if you want to be a pro golfer. In this chapter, I am going to talk about golf swing consistency, the reasons behind inconsistent golf swing, and how you can improve it.

What Does Consistency in Golf Mean?

There is a subtle difference between scoring well and a consistent golf swing that makes solid contact. It is very important for you to know what exactly you are trying to achieve. Only then will you be able to invest your time in the right things.

Here are five key factors that play a huge part in maintaining consistency in the golf swing:

Setup Position

You have already won half of the game if your setup position is on point. That is because every time when you stand over a shot, if your aim is off, then you won't succeed in making consistent contact.

- ***Balance and Grip*** – Although there isn't any particular "correct" way of gripping, you just need to make sure that your gripping positions are the same every time. You should also lay emphasis on the gripping pressure. You should not grip it too tightly, as it will create tension, and you should not grip it too softly either. You should also maintain your posture and balance.

- ***Clubface Alignment*** – Your clubface must be square to the target. If your clubface is not square, you should use a magnetic lie angle tool to make it easier for you to see.

- **Body Alignment** – Focus on your shoulder alignment, hips, and feet. Record yourself while practicing. This will help you to get a better insight.

Rhythm and Tempo

Once you are done with the setting up, it is time for you to focus on the areas of the golf swing that you need to improve. Rhythm and tempo are the two most common areas that golfers need to work on. If you rush your transition or take back the club too fast, it is not going to work that way. The moment you take your club back, you need to start gaining and accelerating your speed constantly.

Jerking the club back aggressively on the backswing is going to cause deceleration on the downswing. The same goes for downswing as well. Take the club back slowly, take a pause, then start swinging the club with power. Start the downswing slowly, and then start accelerating when the club becomes parallel to the ground.

Impact Position

No matter how your backswing is, it won't matter if your impact position isn't right. The club should be lined up with your left arm. It will create a power triangle between the ball and your arms. Your head should be behind the ball. This will help you to get your weight on your forward foot. Then extend it fully past the golf ball. Bow your wrist slightly for compressing the ball and delofting the club.

Not Forgetting Your Short Game

Even the finest golfers hit poor shots at times. If you have a good short game, then you will be able to disguise the bad shots. You should obviously practice for improving consistency in golf swings, but you shouldn't neglect short games.

Competing Consistently

You will be able to compete consistently on your big day only if you inculcate the right habits. You need to have a proper pre-round routine. For example, you can arrive 30 minutes prior to the game and start warming up. Lack of focus might be a reason behind your inconsistency in scoring well. So, you need to stay focused, and a pre-round routine will help you to do so. You need to avoid swing thoughts and try creating a routine that will empower your game. Lastly, you should not copy others and stick to your own game plan.

Reasons Behind Inconsistent Golf Swing and How You Can Improve It

Improving consistency in your golf swing is a great goal, and this will make golf more enjoyable for you. Here are some reasons behind the inconsistency in your golf swing and some tips on how you can build your consistency.

Your Setup Is Inconsistent

The primary key to good solid contact and balance is good posture. If you can be in a good posture for every club present in your bag, then you will automatically have better consistency in direction and contact. A good posture is bending forward from your hips in a way that your hands stay hanging below your shoulders. You must have a setup routine that you need to repeat with every club you have. For example, grip your club and then step forward using your trailing foot. Then bend down from your hips to set your club behind the golf ball and then aim to the target. If you have this kind of setup routine, it will help you have a good setup with all the clubs you have.

Issues of Clubface

A square clubface can help to build a great consistency even when the contact is not perfect. The miss is often really straight. So, if your misses are playable, it will automatically boost your confidence level. An overly open or an overly closed clubface will force you to make compensation within your swing. As a result, this might lead to inconsistency in your golf swing. Making grip adjustment is really uncomfortable, but it will surely help you to get the desired ball flight. Once you see an improvement in the ball flight, the discomfort will also seem lesser.

You Are Losing Balance

If you lose your balance right after making a perfect golf swing, your perfect golf shot might get ruined. It is surprising that a lot of golf players don't even realize that they are off-balance and that they are failing to hold their finishing position. You should record it to identify your lack of balance. You must hold your finish position until the ball stops moving. You might feel that it is easy, but that is certainly not the case. It is way difficult than you think. You might think that you have already hit the ball, and so it won't matter much if you don't hold your position. This thought is going to get you in trouble. If you lose your balance while finishing your swing, it suggests that you are also off-balance during your swing.

You are Using Clubs that Don't Provide Enough Forgiveness

A lot of golf players don't find the club face's center every time. Spray some powder on the clubface, and you will notice that the contact point mainly moves around the center of clubface for most golfers. Golf clubs that provide a lot of forgiveness are very helpful. It is recommended to have a set of clubs that are designed to provide enough forgiveness. Try the clubs, and you will surely find the one that is perfect for you.

You Didn't Do Enough Practice Swings

You can carry a maximum of 14 clubs in your bag. If all of them are of different lengths, that might lead to inconsistency. Practice swings will help you to get accustomed to the length of the club that you are using. In case the ball is present on the ground, then the club will also brush the grass. If you switch to a longer club without taking enough practice swings, you might end up hitting the ground too much. On the other hand, if you switch to a shorter club without taking enough practice swings, you might end up hitting a thin shot. This happens because you are not accustomed to the changing length of the club. It is highly recommended that you take enough practice swings until you get comfortable with the clubs you will use during the real match. It will surely improve your consistency.

You Aren't Hitting the Ground

At first, you need to understand how a golf ball gets lifted up into the air. If you don't understand that, there will surely be inconsistency in your golf swing. A lot of golfers enter this sport after coming from another sport. For example, the way of hitting a ball in a tennis game and a golf game are totally different. So, a golfer who isn't accustomed to this sport might get uncomfortable with hitting the ground for lifting the ball up because their concept is totally different. So, when your golf ball is on the ground, it is important for you to hit the ground during both practice swings and real matches.

You Aren't Working on Your Weaknesses

Hitting solid shots is obviously more fun, but it is obvious that there are certain shots that some golfers might not like. Your weaknesses might show up when you are under stressful situations or during your competitive rounds. You need to identify these weaknesses while you play. This will help you to have a better understanding of where you should focus and the areas you need to work on. Everyone has weaknesses, but not everybody struggles to overcome them. It is recommended that you get help from your golf instructor about how you can improve your technique and how you can work on your weaknesses.

You Aren't Practicing Smart

Practicing for a long time doesn't help much. What you really need here is a smart practice. Only then will you be able to work on your skills and confidence. There are a lot of golfers who have no clue about how long they should practice. Technique building practice is generally more repetitive, as here you are working through a change. Feedback from an outside aid or a ball will be really helpful in this situation. Once you have developed a reasonable technique, practice it to improve consistency. It is recommended that you take help from experts for making your individual practice plan.

You Don't Have a Good Understanding of Cause and Effect

A lot of golfers keep repeating the same mistakes over and over again. That is because they don't even understand what is actually causing the miss. Practicing repeatedly and making the same mistakes isn't what you should do. You should understand what is causing the miss in the first place and what was wrong with your ball flight. Then you need to evaluate the things that you do that might be responsible for the miss. After figuring out all these, you need to focus on making the necessary adjustments. For example, suppose you are aware of your weaknesses like you don't want your ball flight to be too high, or the fact that you have a tendency to position the ball way too centered and that you can't tilt your shoulder back enough, etc. Knowing all these is extremely helpful because you get to know the exact areas you need to work on.

You React a Lot to Bad Shots

Even the best golfers out there hit bad shots sometimes. It is completely natural. What keeps them going is the fact that they don't overreact to these things. If you are someone who overreacts after every bad shot, then you need to change this immediately. This is very harmful to you as it will only deteriorate your game. You should try to under-react after your bad shots. Just take the ball and keep trying. If you see that you are continuously struggling, then you need to adjust your game plan a little. The most important thing is to remain calm. This will prevent you from losing your mind and making bad decisions. Stay calm, take the right decisions, make necessary adjustments, and keep trying.

I'm pretty confident that if you follow these tips, you will find yourself having a consistent golf swing in no time.

Chapter 5: Setting the Right Spine Angle

Setting the right spine angle is your key to becoming professional at taking an effortless swing that is not compromising on the distance and at the same time is both accurate and impactful. So, to become good at taking a swing or to become a good golfer in general, you need to learn to get your spine angle right.

There are few other reasons as to why you need to get your spine angle right, they are:

1. When you have the right spine angle, then it acts as the foundation. Once you have a solid foundation, then it can work as a stable centerline for the swing (the rotation).

2. It helps golfers to achieve balance while taking the golf swing.

3. As you are taking the swing, there is the generation of a strong centrifugal force. Unless and until you have the right spine angle, this enormous force that gets generated while taking the swing can hurt your back. Thus it is important to have the right spine angle to avoid back pains.

In this chapter, I will be discussing the various spine angles that golfers can maintain to improve their game and their golf posture and few common mistakes as well. So, continue reading to learn about the different ways through which you can get the right spine angles and the different ways by which you can improve your posture while playing golf.

The Correct Spine Angle While Addressing the Golf Ball

A golfer needs to bend or tilt forward their upper body to get the right spine angle while addressing the golf ball. The bending can depend on the amount of flex that the golfer applies on the knees. The gradient between the torso and the player's legs will help determine the stability of the player's feet and speak about whether or not the spine angle is right.

Depending on the flex that is set on the knee, the golfer will either bend their upper body much or less. However, the optimum position where the spine angle is just right is when the golfer is bending the upper half of their body somewhere between the extremes, which is the middle ground between bending too much or bending too less, and it seems like the golfer is almost standing straight.

When the golfer is not bending the upper half of the body much, then he or she will be said to be standing tall—standing tall while addressing means that the gradient between the upper body and the legs will be greater or the maximum. In this technique, the knees will only be bent slightly. To get a clearer picture of this posture, you may imagine yourself to be sitting on a stool. The posture is almost similar to what you find your body in when you are seated on a stool - the knees are not bent that deep, and there is a slight bent on the upper half of the body. This real-life example was proposed by Ben Hogan, and the addressing technique can also be referred to as reduced forward bend. This position can be a little on the edge as a slight change will cause the torso to be upright, thus making the player standing too tall, and that does not make for a desirable spine angle.

Now that you are standing tall, if from that position you forward bend your upper body a bit more, then that will be the average or normal spine angle. There will be flex on both knees. At this average forward bend position, you can address easily and most comfortably.

As at the normal bend position, your golf club will be addressing the ball comfortably; it is recommended for all golfers. This is the default bending position where the golfers can easily swing their golf clubs without inducing much muscle tension. The relaxed addressing is possible because, at this angle, the central axis of the golfer is at the center and moves down till the feet.

The entire body weight is now completely shifted to the center of the axis of the body, and there is no muscle tension. The feet will also have a stronghold on the ground, making the position very stable. The posture will allow golfers to have the most effective swings as the feet are stable on the ground and thus allowing for a smooth rotation of the upper body.

There is another possibility where the golfer might bend their torso a bit too much. The position or structure where the golfer is bending their torso way too much can be referred to as a severe forward bend. Severe forward bending can be easily observed as the golfer will look as if he or she is bending down to reach out to something that is on the ground.
Since the golfer is bending their body way too much, the gradient or angle between their bodies and legs will be very small since they lie close to

one another. This stance is not desirable at all as the central axis of the body is not right, and thereby it will cause unnecessary muscle tension. This muscle tension might prove severe as they are capable of causing back pain to the players.

To conclude, there can be three broad categories of forwarding bending of the torso depending on the flex on both the knees while addressing. The normal forward bend, the reduced forward bend, and lastly, the severe forward bend - out of these, the default posture includes the average forward bend. The normal forward bend allows the golfers to address most comfortably out of all the other postures, and the spine angle is just right. The severe forward bend is what all golfers should refrain from practicing.

Getting the Spine Pattern Right

Now having set the spine angle right, you must also set the spine pattern right. The idea behind setting the spine pattern right is that you must be able to rotate comfortably while making the golf swing. There are three spine patterns to chose from for the golfers, out of which two are not desirable, and only one of them should be practiced.

STRAIGHT LINE   C - SHAPE   S - SHAPE

The three broad categories of spine patterns available for golfers to chose from are:

1. The S shape spine pattern

2. The C shape spine pattern and

3. The Straight Line spine pattern

Now let us take a look at all the spine patterns in detail and find out the optimal one and discuss ways of correcting the postures that are wrong or not desirable.

The S-Shape Spine Pattern

The S-shape spine pattern is also referred to as the S posture mistake. It is perhaps one of the most common mistakes made by many golfers. In this posture, the golfer bends the torso and sticks out the rear end in such a way to make the shape 'S.' The tail bone of the golfer making the posture is lined up in the middle of their back.

Usually, the spine angle made by the golfer is the standing tall angle or the reduced forward bend, and the rear end is stuck out exaggeratedly. Due to the placements, there is a slight or deep depression at the back of the player.

Due to this trench at the lower back, the entire or the maximum weight of the body is placed on the lower spine, but it is supposed to be placed at the hips. Thus, there is a distraction while taking the rotation during the golf swing. The distraction is due to the disturbance in the axis of rotation and the build-up of muscle tension in the lower back region.

Due to the muscle tension, the golfer might even have to stop midway through completing the golf swing in case of severe pain. The S-shape spine pattern is bad for golf club swing and for health as due to the awkward lower back posture, there can be severe back pain. So it is better to abstain from setting this pattern in your gameplay, but if by chance it is encountered, then the posture can be fixed by strengthening the core muscles.

The C Shape Spine Pattern

The C shape spine pattern or the c posture mistake is caused when the player is slumping their shoulders in such a way that their torso makes the C shape. The player looks as if he or she is hunching, and this posture too shifts the weight of the upper half of the body to the lower back.

Players can encounter the posture due to various reasons, such as if the player is not putting in enough effort to keep their back straight during the address due to lack of proper instruction, weak abdominal, short clubs, or the imbalance of muscles in the lower or upper body. Due to the rounding of the shoulders and the back due to exaggerated shoulder bend, the player will lack energy or strength.

The golfer will likely have to hold the golf club down to the ground, next to the ball. This is not a good posture and looks lousy as well. The golf swing is also not going to be completely effective due to the shifting of the weight to the lower back.

As the weight of the body is shifted to the lower spine region of the player, they will likely get exhausted. The optimum way of getting a comfortable swing is having a proper axis of rotation, which is again possible if the weight is evenly distributed through the body, that is, from the back through to the hips and down to the feet.

So there are two severe mistakes with the C posture - the weight of the body is placed in the wrong region, and due to the exaggerated bending of shoulders, the proper energy and swing are disrupted. The rotation can never e smooth, and there will be occasional stops due to exhaustion. This is thus another severe mistake that golfers need to try to avoid, as otherwise, they will have to face severe back pain after their game.

The Straight Line Spine Pattern

Out of all the patterns, the straight-line pattern is the optimal spine pattern. With proper guidance and practice, this pattern can be easily achieved. As the name suggests, the straight-line pattern makes a straight line considering the back of the player, the tail bone, and the hips.

It includes no slumping or exaggerating body postures. The golfer simply needs to stand with his feet kept apart at a distance equal to the length of his or her shoulder and then keep the back in a straight line. The hips, the tail bone, and the back in between the shoulders are all in the same straight line. The weight of the body is also distributed evenly, causing a proper axis of rotation and thus making room for comfortable and smooth rotation during a golf swing. There is no muscle tension as well, and it allows the golfer to take solid shots.

Getting the Proper Shoulder Alignment

Other than setting the spine angle and spine pattern right, there is another factor that most golfers overlook but should also be taken into consideration. That is getting the proper shoulder alignment. By shoulder alignment, I mean the position of one side shoulder to the other side shoulder.

It is important to get the shoulder placements right as otherwise there will be a crooked spine problem that also leads the golfers to hit consistent fat shots. Both of which are not desirable in the game of golf and life.

The ideal way to align your shoulders is to let them follow the arm placement and movements. It will lead to a slight side tilt which is just the right way to set the shoulder. The ideal shoulder setting is when the left shoulder is tilted slightly upwards than the right shoulder. The right shoulder will be in a straight line with the left shoulder and will be at a lower level too.

Chapter 6: A Step-by-Step Guide for a Proper Grip

Your golf grip can really make or break the shot you are making, and having the correct grip really makes a lot of difference. It improves your performance exponentially, and if your grip is not exactly in place, then your shots can heavily suffer from the same. Whether you are just a beginner when it comes to the game or are an expert, you need to know how you should correctly hold your golf club. Having a good grip is important because if your grip is proper and consistent, it will improve how you are striking the ball and make your performance more regular and consistent. Besides that, a proper grip can also help you fix your slice, increasing the chances that you have a stellar all-around game every time you hit the course.

If you think that it might be a little weird to place so much importance on just the grip in golf, remember the wise words of Ben Hogan - "*Good golf begins with a good grip.*" Many of the greatest ball strikers of the game have vouched having a consistent grip to be the secret of improving their performance when it comes to ball striking. Just think about exactly how many times you would need to hold a golf club in your life. If you are a regular player, then the answer to this might be in thousands or even tens of thousands.

If you are going to do something so frequently and for so many times, would you not want to make sure that you are doing it right? If you want to waste less time in figuring out how to hold your club and focus more on bettering your shots instead, you will need to get your perfect golf grip in place. That is exactly what this chapter will help you out with. Read on to find out some of the easiest and most effective tips and tricks to improve your golf grip –

Assess the Grip You Currently Have

You cannot work on improving your grip if you are not devoting some time to first figuring out what might be wrong with your current grip, which might be negatively affecting your performance. This is why, before getting all technical and dissecting grip sizes and techniques, we need to start from the very basics. Unless you are an absolute pro with years and years of impeccable experience, the chances are that your grip would need some help because there is room for improvement. The first step to improving your grip is to accept the fact that the grip you currently have is perhaps not the perfect one.

Get yourself started with picturing this - you are about to tee off, or you are trying to stick your shot close while on a short par 3. What do you visualize? How are you holding your club? Where are your fingers, and how is your knuckle positioned? How comfortable do you feel, and most importantly, how comfortable are you about making a perfect shot?

How do you see your performance pan out if you were to make your shot given your current preferences? Do you think you would be able to make the perfect shot every time, or is there some room for improvement here? If yes, then great, we can get started right away!

Position Your Hand Properly

Once you have picked your golf club up, the first thing you need to do is to figure out how to hold it, that is, how to position your hand around your club. Before you pick your club up, put your weaker hand out (your non-dominant hand, which would be left for a right-handed golfer), and use it to pick the club. Now, turn your hand over in a way that helps you see both the knuckles of your weaker hand. Once this has been set, notice the V shape which your thumb and index finger are making, and point this shape towards the shoulder of your dominant hand (which is the right shoulder here).

You need to make room for around half an inch of your golf club to peek out from the top of your grip, so position your fingers accordingly. Next, the thumb of your left finger needs to point down the right-hand side of the shaft of your golf club. After this, use your right hand to grip your club in a way that has the thumb of your right-hand position on the top of your left thumb. Make sure that your right thumb is comfortably sitting over the left side of the shaft, and also check whether it faces downwards or not.

Do not freak out or panic if all of this sounds a little too much or too intimidating for you and if you feel that even after following this, you do not feel the most comfortable with how your hand has been positioned. You are only just getting started, and if you feel like you cannot do all of it on your own, then you can perhaps turn to molded grip trainers. These can help you out as they are appropriately molded to guide you regarding exactly where your hands, thumbs, and other fingers need to rest when you are fixing your grip. You can even think of pairing a molded grip trainer with another tempo trainer. A portable, convenient tempo trainer can be carried around with you and can be placed anywhere so that you can pack in some of those extra practice swings, which will boost your confidence and get you all ready once you hit the course.

Check the Size of Your Grip

To know how your hand must be positioned on your club, you need to have some knowledge about grip wraps and grip sizes. All your clubs come with a rubberized grip on them, and these grips would all be of a standardized size. However, these sizes are not universal, and although they are standardized, you might still be using a grip that is not the correct size for you. If you need to change your grip, start by seeing what other size groups are available for you to use and whether any of those would suit your grip better or not.

There are grips that come in different sizes-standard, mid-size, over-size, and so on- with all the sizes having multiple measurements under their umbrella. This means that many times, your actual problem might not even be your grip, it could just be that you are using the wrong grip, and your current grip would be absolutely accurate if you have adopted a different-sized grip for your golf club.

For the time being, stick to the size you have and try to test out if that is the right one for you. Read this entire guide and then make a call about if you are in need of a different size or not.

In case you find yourself repeatedly slicing or pulling- in spite of already having fixed the way you are holding your club- it might be the case that you need a different size for your grip. You might want to visit a trusted golf club shop to get some advice on which size to select for yourself, and the exact size would, of course, depend on how your hands are shaped and sized. You might need a smaller grip than your current one if you have short fingers and thin, petite hands, but on the other hand, if your hands are more large and firm, it might be time to look for a bigger size.

Make a Grip Mark

Bring your Sharpie (or whatever your trusted brand of permanent, water-resistant markers is) out and get ready to make a mark! When you are packing your golf kit or your practice bag, make sure to pack a marker along with you at all times. If you are not completely confident about how your golf club fits into the nook of your right hand, you can whip your marker out and use it to draw two lines over your gloves.

You need to mark these lines over the correct angles so that they can serve as a handy guide whenever you are a little unsure. These marks will help remind you how the club should be positioned in your grip, and it will also give you some motivation as it will remind you that you are on the right track and are not miscalculating your shot. If you are worried about breaking any rules by using this extra help, do not worry! It does not go against any professional guidelines. It is perfectly acceptable to mark your golf gloves, and it is very similar to how some players might mark their golf balls to start the putt on line.

Check the Pressure of Your Grip

Besides the size of your grip, pressure is another variable which you need to keep in check. How hard you hold your golf club is crucial to learning how to shape your strikes. You must not hold on to your club too firmly for the knuckles of your finger to turn almost white. Do not forget that you are only playing a sport for fun and not holding on to dear life on a rollercoaster. Do not stress your hands out.

However, this does not mean that you should hold the club too gently as well as if your grip is too light, you might lose all your control over the golf club, and it can slip out of your grip. Position your hands in a way so that it grips the golf club softly yet firmly rough so that you are comfortable and your arms are relaxed. In this position, move the club around slightly to check if it is in position. It also helps shake off any tension in your arms and prepares you better for making the perfect shot.

Interlocking and Overlapping

There are two different ways in which you can shape your grip out – interlocking and overlapping (or overlocking). This depends on, as the name suggests, whether you are locking your hands together using your fingers over your club or not. Some players choose to interlock their hands while some players do not, and both of the techniques work absolutely fine! There is no fixed or preferred way to do this. You just need to see which one works better for you and stick to that.

Having said that, using the interlock method by linking both of your hands together has emerged to be a somewhat more prevalent choice among most golfers of late. This has become the more preferred choice since an interlocked grip helps promote a better wrist grip and hinge and also makes your overall grip firmer in nature.

The most commonly used method of linking your fingers is the overlapping grip, also known as the Vardon grip. What happens with this is that you need to grip your hands by joining them together in a way that the little finger of your right hand is situated in-between the middle finger and the index finger of your left hand. Once that is in place, you have to align your left thumb towards the middle of the palm of your right hand and then proceed with making your shot.

Now that you have gone through the most common tips to figure out your perfect grip for a game of golf get started! See what size, pressure, and linking techniques work for you, and choose only the strategies that help make your game better and your posture more comfortable. Your grip should not be one that makes you compromise on either your performance or your comfort, and by following these suggestions, you are bound to reach a convenient middle ground which will only make you fall even more in love with the game.

Chapter 7: Exercises for Improving Body Coordination Skills

When it comes to the golf swing, the sequencing of the swing with absolute efficiency and the right amount of power is extremely important and maybe more important than absolute strength. When we are talking about athletics, the success rate of a person depends upon the speed and sequence that he is using. Through these sequences, the impulses in his\her body are getting transmitted to achieve the desired body action. The thing about golf is that it is such a sport that might not seem to be needing a lot of physical exertion as it doesn't seem to be predominantly physical, but the player needs to look after a certain level of flexibility and fitness so that he\she can meet the daily challenges that come in the golf course. The more the body's coordination skills improve, the easier it will be for that player to concentrate physically and mentally as all the senses will be invested in making that shot a good one. Let us then look at some of the ways in which proper exercising can be done to improve a person's body coordination skills while keeping in mind the challenges that can come and could be avoided in a golf swing.

Certain fundamental skills need to be mastered if the physical development of the golfer is to be kept in mind. These skills will help improve the grip, stance, and alignment of the golf swing. These are the basics, which must be checked when on the golf course so that no compensations are needed to be made elsewhere in the swing. The skills are –

- Upper Body Rotation.

- Hip Rotation.

- Pelvic Tilt.

- Hip Hitch.

- Standing Hip Flexion.

- Deep Overhead Squat.

- Upper Body Postural Control.

Upper Body Rotation

When a golfer is performing a backswing, he\she needs to rotate his\her upper body on their lower body. This particular movement helps a golfer to do that correctly, without hurting themselves. The Upper Body Rotation movement helps the golfer to correct posture during a swing so that a correct sequence of body parts is engaged. The proper posture is maintained during the shot to produce consistency and power.

If you are a golfer, you need to have proper coordination in your abdominal muscles in order to do an upper body rotation. At the same time, you need to have an adequate amount of flexibility in your lateral trunk muscles and in your upper back region for the movement.

How to Practice It?

- Lay on your back and put your feet comfortably on the ground. Next, you need to straighten your arms and put your fingertips together.

- After that, rotate your chest while all the time maintains a triangle between your arms and your chest.

- As you are doing this, keep your knees pointed up throughout.

- Try to reach as far as possible, that is, rotate as far as possible while making sure that your body posture is correct and you are not losing balance.

Hip Rotation

If you want to achieve a correct hip posture when you are taking a swing, you need to be able to rotate your hips independently of your upper body. This movement helps you get that. When taking a swing, you need to develop a certain amount of power to maintain the correct body sequence. This movement will help you with that and will assist you in transitioning smoothly from the backswing into the downswing.

If you are to do this properly, then you need to be able to coordinate your deep pelvic and abdominal muscles in order to produce rotation and, at the same time to have an adequate amount of flexibility that will allow your hips and gluteal muscles to rotate properly.

How to Practice It?

- Stand in your golf posture with your hands placed securely at the back of support.

- Next, keep in mind to keep your upper body fixed and try to rotate your hips in a swiveling motion.

- It is important to keep this posture of you maintained at all times, so keep that in mind.

- It is important to note that they must rotate about your spine while you are rotating your hips and not tilt from side to side.

- As and when you become more comfortable and competent in this exercise, go to the next level, which is, take your hands off the support and place them on your chest and repeat the same thing, keeping in mind to maintain your posture.

Pelvic Tilting

This pelvic tilting movement will help you rock and tilt your pelvis in relation to your trunk. This movement will also help you develop a balance between your abdominal and your back muscles. It will help you to position your spine correctly in the address position. In order to do this correctly, you need to position and coordinate your abdominal muscles in order to produce tilting of the pelvis. Your hips and your gluteals should be adequately flexible to allow this tilting.

As a golfer, you need to develop core strength, and this movement will help you get that. It is imperative as a golfer to know your spine and pelvis position so that you can place them in a neutral position and maintain your posture like that. This will help you to perform strengthening exercises without getting injured. When you are in the golf swing, this earlier practice will help you get your positions correct.

How to Practice It?

- Stand in the correct golf posture and rest your hands at the back of support.

- Keep your upper body fully steady and tilt your pelvis under and back.

- Remember to keep your legs still and maintain your golf posture at all times.

- As you slowly get better at this movement, you can increase the frequency of your competence by placing your hands across your chest and keep repeating this movement while you stabilize your upper body and maintain that at all times.

- In case you are having a problem doing this easily, that means you still need to improve your flexibility a bit more and work on your body control.

Hip Hitch

For a good and controlled swing, you need to hitch your hips up and down in a stable manner. This movement will test your ability as a golfer to transfer your weight efficiently – both during the backswing and when you are into the follow-through. Your lateral hip muscles need to have a lot of strength to do this properly, and you need to have a good balance in order to perform this exercise on one leg. Your lateral hip muscle will provide the stability that is needed to generate power when you are performing the swing without excessive swaying and sliding. That is how they create a stable balance for the base necessary for that golf swing.

Your spine will be relieved of a lot of stress with more strength and control in these muscles, and it also helps you maintain posture during the golf swing. This movement is essential for the safety and prevention of any injury that might happen during performance. This technique will help you get accustomed to the advanced training of golf with more practice.

How to Practice It?

- First, stand on the edge of a step and keep the other leg free and hanging while balancing yourself by keeping your fingers on the wall beside you for support.

- Keep at this position and try bending and straightening your knee and raise and also lower your foot.

- This movement should take place at the stance hip, and then you should feel your muscles in the stance hip working.

- As you slowly get more comfortable with this exercise, take it a step forward by doing it on a step but on the ground level with your free leg bent to right angles at the knee up and down as you did previously with your free foot.

Standing Hip Flexion

As a golfer, you need to be able to bend forward at the hips properly, and it is crucial because it will help you take on a correct position and posture, and at the same time, it will help you maintain this posture throughout the swing. This is a relatively simple position, but many-a-time people get it wrong. That can lead to a lot of physical and technical problems, and it is absolutely mandatory to learn this before you get into advanced training. With proper standing hip flexion movement, you will learn how to have a balanced and neutral back position that will help you not develop any back problems and other health issues.

You need to have powerful gluteal muscles at the back of your hips in order for you to do this properly to maintain proper core strength. Your spinal stabilizing muscles also need to be well controlled and balanced for you to do this properly so that you might not get hurt during the movement.

How to Practice It?

- Firstly, you need to stand with a golf club in either hand, with the club resting against your thighs.

- Now keep in mind to maintain your balance at all times, look ahead and try bending forward slowly.

- You might notice your knees bending slightly as you are bending down.

- You need to keep doing this while keeping at your posture. Do not lose balance, and as you continue with this, you might sense a stretch at your hamstrings.

- If you are finding this technique challenging to do, that means you have certain issues with your balance of the body, and you need to practice more.

- In case the difficulty still doesn't go, try kneeling on all fours and keep your hands under your shoulders and keep your knees under your hips.

- After that, arch and round your back, and then try finding a mid-position. It will be the neutral position of your spine.

- Maintain this position and try rocking back and forth as much as you can.

Deep Overhead Squat (DOHS)

As a golfer, you need to squat properly with your arms raised above your head, which is what this movement tests. This technique is extremely important as it will help you maintain the correct posture when you are taking a swing. With this, you will be able to sequence your movements properly, which increases your core strength. You will be at a much lower risk rate if you can properly squat with your arms raised high, as it will decrease the pressure on your lower back. It is essential that you learn this skill soon because a swing requires you to lift your arms up above your shoulder height while maintaining your posture all the time.

You might have poor postural habits in your everyday life, resulting in you having a poor performance in this skill. In order to do this properly, you should be able to coordinate your gluteal muscles to bend at your hips and keep up the correct position of your spine. You will also need good flexibility in your hips, ankles, upper body, knees, and in your lateral trunk muscles.

How to Practice It?

- For this, you need to stand feet shoulder-width apart, and you need to hold a golf club over your head with your elbows bent at right angles.

- You need to be constant in your position and press the golf club as high as possible.

- Try keeping the golf club directly over your ankles and keep your heels on the ground. Then, squat down as low as is possible for you.

- It might be that you are facing problems with this, and that could be for many reasons. You could then try doing this entire process by placing a small raise under your heels.

- You could also try this by placing towels under your feet for better calf flexibility. This is known as a Plantarflexed Deep Overhead Squat.

- In case you lean forward more than you should while doing this, you might feel a tightness of your upper body that will limit you. In that case, place your hands across your chest and try doing this entire process again. This is known as Hands Across Chest Squat. If you see that you can now squat easily, keep in mind that you need to improve a lot on your upper back and your lower trunk flexibility.

Upper Body Postural Control

This technique is helpful to test your ability to control the postural position of your upper body, and that will include your neck, upper back, and shoulders. As a golfer, it will help you adopt and maintain the correct posture needed during a swing. This technique is also useful to maintain a correct swing plane, especially when you are doing a backswing and also while you are transitioning into the downswing.

Like many other basic movements, this one too can be performed wrong easily and as a result of your poor postural habits in your everyday life. The consequence of your wrong postures can be a feeling of tightness in your muscles at the front of your body, such as the pectoral muscles present in your chest and your biceps, and the muscle in the front of your neck. You might feel weakness in the muscles that help you have a good posture, such as the muscles that are present to stabilize your shoulder blades while maintaining the posture of your neck.

How to Practice It?

- You need to stand against a wall with your feet approximately ten centimeters away from the wall. Then, you need to rest your back on the wall.

- Next, you need to flatten your lower back against the wall and remember to maintain this posture throughout the movement.

- After this, you need to raise your arms at right angles to your sides, rest your elbows on the wall properly and then, bent your elbows at right angles with your palms down.

- Keep in mind to keep your shoulder blades back and down and then rotate your forearm back to the wall.

- When the back of your hands is on the wall, you need to draw your head back to the wall while keeping your eyes looking straight ahead.

- In case you are having any difficulty, you might have a problem with your abdominal muscles, and you need to practice more pelvic tilting that we mentioned earlier.

Practicing proper exercises is extremely important when it comes to golf, as improving your body coordination can prove to be extremely helpful in not getting into injuries while maintaining a proper posture. The lack of this might lead to physical pain and injuries, which should be avoided at all costs.

Chapter 8: How to Expand the Length and Width of Your Swing?

There is no doubt about the fact that if the length of your swing becomes longer and if the radius of your sing widens, you will be able to hit the ball farther. The length of the golf swing and the width of the golf swing are two mutually exclusive elements. That means you might have a short wing with good with or even have a long wing with a very little width. There are certain aspects of these two elements that can be related. For example, if you extend your left arm in a certain way, you can achieve both good length and good width in your swing. You don't necessarily need to be a flat-bellied, super-flexible teenager for being able to expand the length and width of your swing. All you need is the right tactics to do so.

Swing Width

The width of the swing is nothing but the radius of your clubhead from the center of your chest or sternum throughout the swing. If the swing width is more, then the distance traveled by the clubhead is also more. It also accounts for an increased clubhead speed. The clubhead speed is responsible for determining the degree of power imparted to the ball. The width of your swing hugely depends on the length of your arms (i.e., your innate flexibility). In case you have longer arms compared to some other golfer, the width of your swing will naturally be more than the width of that other golfer.

Similarly, the swing width also depends largely on the amount of body rotation the golfer is capable of attaining. Stretching your arms out in the backswing as much as possible is not going to help you achieve a greater swing width. If you focus on doing so, you will end up separating the arms from your body. As a result, the coordination will break, thereby stopping them from working together as a unit. There is also a tendency of over-shifting towards the right and a tendency of sliding laterally towards the right. These factors might affect the rhythm and the tempo. Bringing everything together at the impact might be quite challenging.

How to Increase the Width of Your Swing?

Here are some ways by which you can expand your swing width effectively:

Shoulder Rotation

The more your shoulder rotation, the wider your swings are. You need to understand that the shoulders don't remain at the same level on the turn. That is simply because your right shoulder remains lower at the address as your right hand is placed lower on the handle. Anyways, your main aim is to keep the shoulders somewhat on a level. You can do this only if you don't raise your right shoulder while trying to lift up your club, or don't drop the left shoulder down while drawing back the club from the ball.

You need to swing back the club with your left arm fully extended, and then later in the backswing, you will have to hinge your wrists. If you manage to do this, your shoulders will surely be rotating on the same level. When you make a wider swing, you just make a flatter plane for yourself to swing. It means that when you complete your backswing keeping your shoulders on the same level, the shaft of the club will also remain on the same line as your shoulders, sometimes, a little below. Overall, it is a good position that allows you to retain your power and enhance flight control.

Weight Transfer

You will have to transfer your body weight to the right side if you want to widen your backswing. Although, don't exaggerate and shift all of your body weight to your right side. Just focus on not transferring your weight to the outer edge of your right foot, and try to transfer it to the inside of it. If you do this, you will be able to gain maximum width on your backswing.

Lateral Head Movement

It might sound absurd, but you need to be moving your head in the swing. When you swing, your head naturally moves to some extent. You just need to make sure that the movement of your head is natural for ensuring the widening of your swing. Moving your head up and down must be avoided for several reasons. Moreover, moving your head up and down doesn't contribute to widening your swing.

Wrist Hinge

You can achieve a wider swing by prolonging your hinge wrist in the backswing. The more you prolong the hinge wrist, the farther the clubhead goes from your body. When the thumbs are coming towards you, you should not begin hinging your wrists. You can start hinging your wrist when your hands are waist high or past that. It will surely widen your backswing. But if you hinge your wrists early by bending your left arm, then you won't achieve a good width in your golf swing.

Left Arm Extension

You need to completely straighten out your left arm in the backswing. Make sure that the elbow doesn't lock, and the arm isn't stiff. There might be a slight give in your elbow, but overall, your arm needs to be straight.

You can also line up twenty to thirty yards left of your actual target and then swing your club on a path towards the target itself. It will help you understand how the club's path can be controlled and how to get a feel for it.

Forward Swing

In addition to the back swinging concept, there is a concept of forward swinging as well. A forward swing component is related to the backswing. It is all about how you are using your elbows. Forward swinging helps you attain the desired width in your swing. The concept is simple. You need to focus on maintaining the distance between your elbows at address throughout the swing. If your right elbow flies behind you or outwards, a separation gets created, thereby altering the path of the club. In case your left elbow flies behind you or outwards at impact, you will end up losing most of the power as well as control over the flight of the ball.

Swing Length

If the length of your swing is long, then the degree of travel of your clubhead is also more. When you take a full swing, and the shaft of the club reaches a point where it becomes parallel to the ground, it roughly goes through 270 degrees. For example, imagine a golfer with his club behind the ball at the address at 6 o'clock position. After swinging the club to parallel, it reaches the 3 o'clock position. So, it has moved 270 degrees. You should not be swinging your club to a 1 o'clock position or a 2 o'clock position because that won't be parallel. If your club moves beyond parallel and tips almost at the ground, then it is past parallel. If you don't have enough technique, flexibility, and strength required for controlling the club, you should focus on getting the club to a parallel position to make solid contact with the ball and play accurate shots. If you can do this, you will be generating more clubhead speed and hitting the ball straighter and farther than you do when the club isn't in a parallel position.

There are certain ways by which you can get your club to reach a parallel position, but that won't be very effective in bringing you an added distance. Instead, it will just diminish your flight control. For example, you can bend your left arm to complete your backswing. It might help you to get your club in a parallel position, or even beyond it, but that won't be effective. Always remember that getting the club to a parallel position is not the only thing that is required to lengthen your swing.

How to Increase the Length of Your Swing?

Here are some ways that will help you to gain longer swings:

Wrist Hinge

If you complete your backswing while entirely hinging your wrists, you can achieve maximum swing length. Although, you need to be extremely cautious that you are not hinging beyond your normal motion range. If you do that, then your left hand is going to lose its grip on the club. As a result, you will try to regrip the club, thereby leading to misdirected shots, mishits, and sometimes even an open clubface at the impact.

Hip or Shoulder Rotation

The swinging of your arms and your hip or shoulder rotation must always be in synch. Throughout the entire swing, your arms need to stay in front of your body. Your elbows must retain their distance and should always point down. Having good flexibility is a must if you want to achieve a good swing length with a full shoulder rotation. Full rotation is when your left shoulder moves to the initial position of your right shoulder. In case a golfer is old and has lost flexibility, he can achieve the same results with hip rotation. Hip rotation is not that dependent on your flexibility.

Center Contact

Center contact is significant for golfers. The shot feels great, and it is exactly where you are capable of optimizing your distance. The two most common problems often seen in amateur golfers are –

- They keep hitting the ball all over the clubface.

- They keep hitting the ball on the exact same wrong spot.

When you hit the ball even one inch off of the clubface's center, you lose almost 10% of your distance then and there. Try spraying your club to find out where exactly you are hitting the club face. In case you are hitting towards the toe, it means either your path is more out to in or the distance between you and the ball is too much. In case you are hitting towards the heel, it either means that your path is more in to out or the distance between you and the ball is too less. In case you hit it all over the face, you need to minimize your area. You should begin with smaller pitch shots and then proceed to work on center contact. Just focus on hitting the club's center and knowing where exactly you need to hit it on the face.

Swinging Faster

Speeding up your swings is a must, and for that, you need to practice faster swings. Your main aim is getting comfortable with faster swings and holding your finish. Out of control swinging will take you nowhere. Take a 7 iron and try swinging the club faster than you usually do. Try swinging the club about ten times. After each swing, take a little pause and then start over. Try to hold your finish. For example, if you are used to swinging at 80mph, try practicing at 85mph. You might end up increasing your speed to 83mph.

Shaft Lean

A lot of golfers find it very difficult to work on their shaft lean. Your main aim is to get your shaft lean more forward than what it was while starting. A lot of golf players have their shaft lean backward at the impact. As a result, the loft gets added, and the contact with the ball also gets affected. A lot of pro golfers turn their 7 iron into a 5 or 6 iron, whereas a lot of amateur golfers do the exact opposite, i.e., they turn a 7 iron into a 9 or 8 iron. Even if you don't swing faster, you can gain distance by improving your impact.

Longer Hand Arc

Here, the concept is that you will be hitting the ball farther if you are taking your hands back farther. If the arc is long, then you will be hitting the ball farther. Lifting your arms or just picking up the club farther isn't going to do you any good. You should do it with your turns. Focus on making a bigger shoulder turn or a bigger hip turn. Your left heel might come off the ground.

Using the Ground

Good footwork is going to help you achieve more length. The ground acts as a power source for the golf players. You can start practicing it at home first. All you have to do is take a club and start swinging back and forth. Feel the weight moving from side to side. Try lengthening the swing while keeping the movement going from side to side. While doing bigger swings, allow your heels to come up and allow yourself to push off of the ground on every swing.

Upgrading Equipment

The right clubhead design, material, length, and weight can help you in swinging faster. As a result, you can achieve longer swings. Upgrade your equipment accordingly!

Hitting the Gym

Being fit isn't a necessity for a golfer, but it indeed is a bonus. Almost all of the pro golfers are very conscious about their fitness as it largely benefits their game. Working out improves your injury prevention, coordination, strength, and flexibility, all of which are important in achieving a good swing length.

Better Sequence

You should have a good sequence in your swing. All the pro golfers have good sequence and power. Take a 7 iron in your right hand and turn it upside down. Put your feet together. When you swing back your club with your right hand, take a side step towards the target using your left foot just when your hand is about rib high. When you do this, you will feel the urge to pull down your right arm. Do this for almost ten swings and then take a normal stance after turning the club over. Then swing back the club. You will feel the step happening, but make sure not to take the step. This will surely improve your sequence.

Faster Tempo

You can gain length in your swing by having a faster tempo. Sometimes, golfers are suggested to slow down and swing slower. But if you swing slowly, you won't be gaining any distance. Increasing the tempo of your swing will lead to an increased swing speed and eventually an increased swing length. Try speeding up your backswing. This will help you to gain speed in your downswing as well.

Changing the Golf Ball

Different kinds of materials are used for making golf balls. Some golf balls are good at higher speeds, whereas some are not. You need to have a significant clubhead speed for compressing a golf ball for optimizing your distance with the ball. There are some balls that go farther, but some spin is sacrificed around the greens. You can even try hitting the ball shorter, and you will have better control around the greens. You should decide what is important for you and what exactly works for you and then move on to selecting your golf ball.

I hope this chapter has been able to better equip you with strategies that are going to help you expand the length and width of your swing.

Chapter 9: Follow These Steps to Increase Your Golf Shot Accuracy

Before we learn a few ways to improve our golf shot accuracy, let us begin by understanding what accuracy is and its importance in the golf swing. The term accuracy in golf denotes the golfer's ability to hit the ball closer to their chosen target. Therefore, accuracy is important for one to have a successful golfing experience. To be able to hit accurate shots and place the ball at perfect places on the golf course makes the golfing experience all the more pleasurable and successful. Therefore, both regular golfers and beginners need to improve in this area to improve their scores. Accuracy does not come overnight, and it requires some practice before you can lower your scores.

Mistakes That Affect the Accuracy

Golf is a sport that does not just depend on technique but needs a lot of time, patience, and practice to master. Even players with experience sometimes falter, so if you are an amateur trying to improve your scores, find out the cause that is preventing you from making the perfect shot. The most common reason is the accuracy, but sometimes an imperfect swing may be the cause. However, accuracy plays an important role in ensuring a good shot, so it is always good to work and improve on it. Listed below are few common mistakes that may affect the accuracy.

- **Going in too hard with the swing** - Amateur golfers often make the mistake of swinging more than they need to. Those who are new to the game commonly understand distance to be a more important factor, thereby swinging more powerfully than required for an average shot. Going all out with the swing may prove to be detrimental because it may affect your balance, and often one loses control of the swing. It prevents one from hitting the shot with their maximum effort and even disrupts the swing's timing. With your timing and balance being off, it is most likely that the shot will be off the line too. Instead of swinging with all your might, be judicious in choosing the right club for the right shot. With a six iron in your bag, it is unnecessary to try and force a seven iron in your target. Once you can get out of the habit of swinging hard, you will see your accuracy to have improved.

- **An imperfect aim** - The most common mistake that golfers make is to think that their swing was off when they hit a ball out of the line. A wrong swing may cause the ball to change direction but what most commonly happens is that the aim was not perfect from the starting. Improving your aim will visibly bring about improvement in your accuracy without working much on your swing. Aiming accurately requires persistent practice and may not be an exciting thing for beginners but mastering it will prove beneficial in the long run in your golfing ventures. Focus on improving the accuracy of your aim by paying little more attention to the driving range.

- **Hitting the ball high** - High shots are good and can be impactful in making a perfect shot. High shots are effective to stop the movement of the ball quickly after it lands, but it is wrong to think that they are always beneficial. This is another common mistake made by golfers, as high shots by many amateurs are considered to be the singular way of landing a perfect shot. In a situation where there is more space for you to work in, it is more likely to lack accuracy if you hit the ball higher. Lower shots have their benefits. You can take some of the side spins off the shot and also prevent the ball from getting affected by the wind when you hit a lower shot. While practicing, it is advisable to practice both higher and lower shots so that you may have both ready at your disposal to apply according to the requirement while playing on the golf course.

- **Not paying attention to the role that lies play** - The lie must be taken into consideration when playing golf as it can determine the perfection of the shot you hit. When you begin with a flawless lie, that is, when to begin each whole you get to position the ball on a tee; there will be no restriction on your accuracy, but once the ball is out of the tee, it is possible to have lies that are of different kinds, and they may be of any number. It is possible to be in a divot, or the ball in the rough may get wind up, you could land in a side-hill lie and many more of such possibilities. Every shot requires you to focus and judge your lie to be able to tell the accuracy of the shot. It is more difficult to have control over the rough when playing from the rough, so it is advisable to keep some amount of gap to make a mistake. If you have an accurate lie in the center of the fairway, then a good swing can yield you an accurate outcome. An integral part of bettering your game is assessing the lie and acknowledging its importance.

There could be many other mistakes that can deter you from being accurate while playing golf, but these are the most commonly made mistakes. Staying away from the above-mentioned errors will help you launch your shots closer to your targets.

Steps to Improve Accuracy

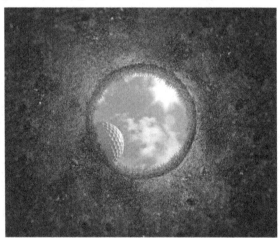

Now that we have already discussed the errors that can prevent accuracy let us learn some points that can help us improve the accuracy.

- The method of approaching the golf ball is primary to attaining accuracy. Amateurs make the mistake of placing their feet next to the ball before placing their clubs in the right position. One must always position the head of the club before positioning their feet. To do so, roll up the ball and then, with its head down, place the club. Before you position your feet, aim the club, or else your feet will likely be placed in the wrong direction. This ensures a good shot which otherwise may be ruined even if there are no mistakes in the alignment of the club face.

- You may take the help of aligning sticks to position your feet better so that you can master the positioning of the club face and your feet at the target. This may take some time, but it is advisable to steadily, taking some time, position your feet and the club face. This is one of the more fruitful tips to improve your golfing ventures, as even with a great swing, your ball may race in the wrong direction if your feet and club are not placed correctly.

- Be careful about the flex in your left wrist at impact. The palm moves closer to your forearm when you bend your wrists. While doing this, the club face must be in the correct position to be able to compress the ball and manage the distance and the route of the ball. You can practice this outside the course with fifty-yard wedge shots till you get this correct.

- The positioning of the knee is a key factor that can determine the accuracy of your shot. A proper weight transfer is essential to establishing a good contact, or else it will result in losing accuracy. This can be fixed by focusing on one thing at a time. First, carefully complete the backswing and then to move your weight to your hips, go down by making a side turn of your hips. You will know that you have made the right weight transfer if you find your right knee pointing at the ball or maybe a little in front of the ball while making the impact.

- Your ability to control the ball also determines your consistency in hitting the target. To improve this, practice swinging for low-lying shots. Take either your lob or a sand wedge and grip it with the left hand. Place the ball at the middle of the stance and transfer very little weight to the left side of your body. Then, swing your arm to a 45-degree position and then proceed to swing down at the back of the golf ball. The grass of the golf course will ensure to limit the follow-through.

- You may hit the ball high or low, but your ball's landing may differ from your aim due to the impact of the wind. Adjusting your swing speed will help you control the trajectory of the ball. Make a slow swing to make a lower shot, and the other way of doing so is by choking down on the club. When you desire a height to your shot, go for a faster swing. The backspin from the faster swing will make the ball fly higher. The way you release can also determine the trajectory of your shot. If you desire to lower the shot, extend your arm while increasing the height; in the follow-through, let the club up more.

- It is imperative to improve your visualization method if you want to improve the accuracy of your shot. The primary cause of a poor drive is a lack of good visualization of the shot. It is not enough to have a general sense of where you want the ball to land up. Fix the spot first where you want the ball to land, then try imagining a circular ring about ten to twenty yards ahead of the target line as if your ball would sail onto the target spot through that ring. This method will give you two spots of visualization that will help in both ways – control the placement of the landing of the ball and the way it gets in there.

- It can happen that when you make contact with the golf ball, it can result in a slice. This may also happen in case of an unstable swing, even though your club face positioning may be correct. What is called the box drill helps with this problem. Stand on the side of a ball box, taking its top half. Then lining up the box parallel to the target line makes a path to facilitate the passage of the shaft just over the box. Keep the box ahead of the ball and try to hit without making contact with the ball to help with the slice.

These are very small changes that, if made, can improve your accuracy and, with regular practice, will bring about progress in your golf skills.

Chapter 10: Quick Swing Fixes That You Should Know About

Are you a beginner at playing golf and looking for tips to improve your game? Then you need to master the swing. It is quite frustrating not to get the hits right. If you want to be a pro golfer, you need to have a perfect swing. Also, the tempo must be right. These factors will determine whether your swings are going to produce the worse rounds or the best round. The ratio between the backswing time and the downswing time is approximately 3:1 for almost all professional golfers. The ratio remains the same irrespective of other factors. If your ratio is right, you will easily get the shots. Whether you are a beginner or a pro, perfecting your swings is a must for advancing in the game.

Find out the reasons behind your poor hits and try eliminating them. Practicing consistently is the key to make perfect golf swings. Always remember that both your body and your mind play a significant role in making the perfect shots. Here are some quick golf swing fixes that you should start implementing for getting the perfect shots.

The Slice

Eliminating the slice requires the clubface to be open to the path of the golf swing. Professionals say that you can use your wristwatch to eliminate a slice. If you are a right-hander and wear your watch on your left hand or a left-hander and wear your watch on your right hand, you have the key to square your clubface. While you are on the downswing, try to roll over the watch face so that it points towards the ground when your club approaches the ball. So, you will be rotating your arms and will be able to effectively eliminate the slice.

The Hook

Try not to hit the ball on its right side. Because if you do, the ball will go in the left direction. You need to close the clubface at impact for pulling this off. In other words, if your clubface comes in

106

contact with the ball's outer half, the ball will go from right to left. If you want to close the clubface at impact, make sure that the clubface comes in contact with the ball's inner side. Select a dimple on the inner side of the ball and try hitting it using the center of your clubface.

The Push

This type of hitting starts right and continues to remain on that line. The problematic part is the fact that the impact is made way too far from the inside. This means that your swinging is more in to out. The body is usually overactive during the starting of the downswing. As a result, it spins open, and the club gets stuck behind the body. Taking a dramatically closed stance is the only way to fix this. Your lower body will be immobilized to make it easier for your arms to catch up and swing past the chest.

The Pull

This type of hitting usually starts left and continues to remain on that side. In this, the clubface is squared to the path, as a result of which, the ball flies straight to the left. This happens when you hit the ball way too hard using your right shoulder and arm. During the start of the downswing, your shoulder makes a jerky movement suddenly towards the ball. As the club is thrown outside, the swinging at the impact is out to in. If you want to avert a pull, you should try to keep your right shoulder back. Make swings using only your right hand and use your left hand to hold back your right shoulder while you swing down. Avoid smashing the ball using your upper body.

The Topped Shot

When you lose your posture or balance, it leads to contact with the ball's upper half, resulting in a top. In this, your hips and your shoulder spin out during the downswing. You can fix this by keeping your head still. For avoiding the spin-out, try resting your left hip on your left foot while swinging. Try picturing your chest pointing towards the ball at impact. This will make sure that you don't lose your posture.

The Toe Hit

When you attempt to swing and release the club early, it results in toe hits where you hit the ball with the club's toe. You need to learn swinging from the inside. For doing this, try placing a second ball inside your iron's heel when you practice. Try swinging with the main ball and try not to hit the second ball. If you practice this, you will learn to swing the club from the inside. This will centralize your strike.

The Heel Hit

Heel hits are mainly of two types. The first type is an off-center hit that moves to the lower right—poor contact results in vibrations that are responsible for causing a stinging sensation in your arms. The second type is the shank. Heel misses are caused mainly due to the exaggerated in to out swinging through the impact. If you want to eliminate this problem, try to make your divots point towards a hair left to your target. Also, try keeping the left wrist flattened through the impact. If you can do this, your heel hits will probably disappear!

The Fat Shot

There is a different weight to a flat shot, but the effect is still the same. In this, the clubhead hits the ground before it hits the ball. For fixing this, the lower part of your swing needs to be moved forward. You need to feel your body weight, and the shaft moved forward at impact. For practicing this, try placing a scorecard approximately 3 inches behind the ball. It needs to be secured to the ground. For doing that, you can use four tees at the corners. Then, try missing the scorecard while swinging into the impact.

The Thin Shot

When the rotation of your chest and hips through the impact stops, it results in a thin shot. As a result, your arms pull in and then get shortened. For fixing this, try making half swings where you purposely look off the ball right before the impact. When you release the eyes towards your target, maintaining full extension through the impact becomes way easier for your arms.

The Whiff

Whiff might result from your anxiety. Sometimes, golfers get too anxious to see the flight of the ball. During a downswing, if you shift to your back foot and allow your arms to collapse through the impact, it pulls your club head upwards in impact. As a result, you might completely miss the ball. If you want to fix this problem, you need to keep a penny in front of the ball and then practice swinging. Try hitting both the ball as well as the penny. This will make the club move on a downward angle. As a result, it will help you in shifting to your front foot.

The Shank

A weak grip is what causes the shank. A soft grip is responsible for leaving the face open at impact, thereby exposing the hosel. You need to strengthen your grip in order to fix a shank. Strengthening your grip helps to square the face at impact. If you stand too close to the ball, it might also cause a shank. Try moving far from the ball till the point you can still make contact.

The Drop-Kick

When the club is coming in at a low angle, and then the clubhead hits the ground before impact, it leaves a shallow divot, thereby resulting in a drop-kick. The primary causes behind these are a bad shift of weight and an improper turn of your shoulder. For fixing this, wear socks and try stimulating your weight shift on a carpeted floor. Practice some swings and try feeling the weight transfer from your right foot's ball to your left foot's ball as you swing through.

The Pop-Up

When your chest is resting too much on your front foot, your weight gets too far forward. As a result, pop-ups happen. If you want to fix this, make sure that your sternum remains behind the belt buckle while setting up with a driver. It helps you swing back and down on the inside path and sweep the ball and doesn't let you chop at it and leave a scrape on your driver's top. You can also try teeing your ball higher. That is because when your chest is moved back, you will hit up on the ball. If you tee higher, this works with your swinging path.

Now that you know these swing fixes, try implementing these, and you will surely start hitting great shots in no time. If you don't have enough practice swings, it is going to be very difficult for you. Practice hitting the ball with these swing fixes and improve your hit.

Since you have reached the end of this book, I hope you apply the principles mentioned here during every shot, and I wish you all the very best for your next game!

Thank you for reading my book, if you have any comments to make, or you want to tell me what you liked and what you did not like, or you simply want to express your opinion on the book you can do it by leaving a short review on Amazon

Made in the USA
Coppell, TX
09 June 2024

33317889R00066